ARF! BEG! CATCH!

This book is for Ann Fleisher, canine spirit
—H.H.

The author gratefully acknowledges the contributions of the following...
Cat, Bill & Maggie Anderson and Stella and Daisy
Boston Aid to the Blind
Anne & Rob Braunstein and Otis
Brookline Animal Care Center
Deborah Bright and Sophie
City of Boston Animal Shelter
Jim Dahlglish and Ol' South's James Dean
Rachel Faith and Max
Ann Fleisher
Shelley Flynn and Amigo
Tom Gearty
Ruth Glicksman and Zeke
Eve and Scott Groper, DVM and Gus
Sonia and Steven Gurevitz and Splashy, Hannah, and Lydia
Peter Jacobson and Ozzy
David Kelley, Kim Pashko, Maloo and Coots
Andreia Lawson Post
Kristyn Leigh and Ulla
Alex MacLean, Kate Conklin and Maggie
Mario
Jennifer Maslow and Harley
Olivia McCullough, Jonathan Sharlin, and Cyan
Amanda Moores and Bosco
Deborah Neswald
Mike O'Bryant and Charlie
Kevin Pertchik and Spanky
Nancy and John Pitas and their mastiffs
Andrea Raynor
Bill Remick, Leslie Wilcox, and Emma
Rob and Andy
Ruth and Eb
Robin Sea
Nir Schu
Winifred S
Hadley Ste
Amy Town and Ollie
Louis "Mala
Deborah, J and Elizabeth Wu and Missy
ZONA, Bo
And all the dogs and people at Ringer Park, Boston,
and Callahan Park, Framingham

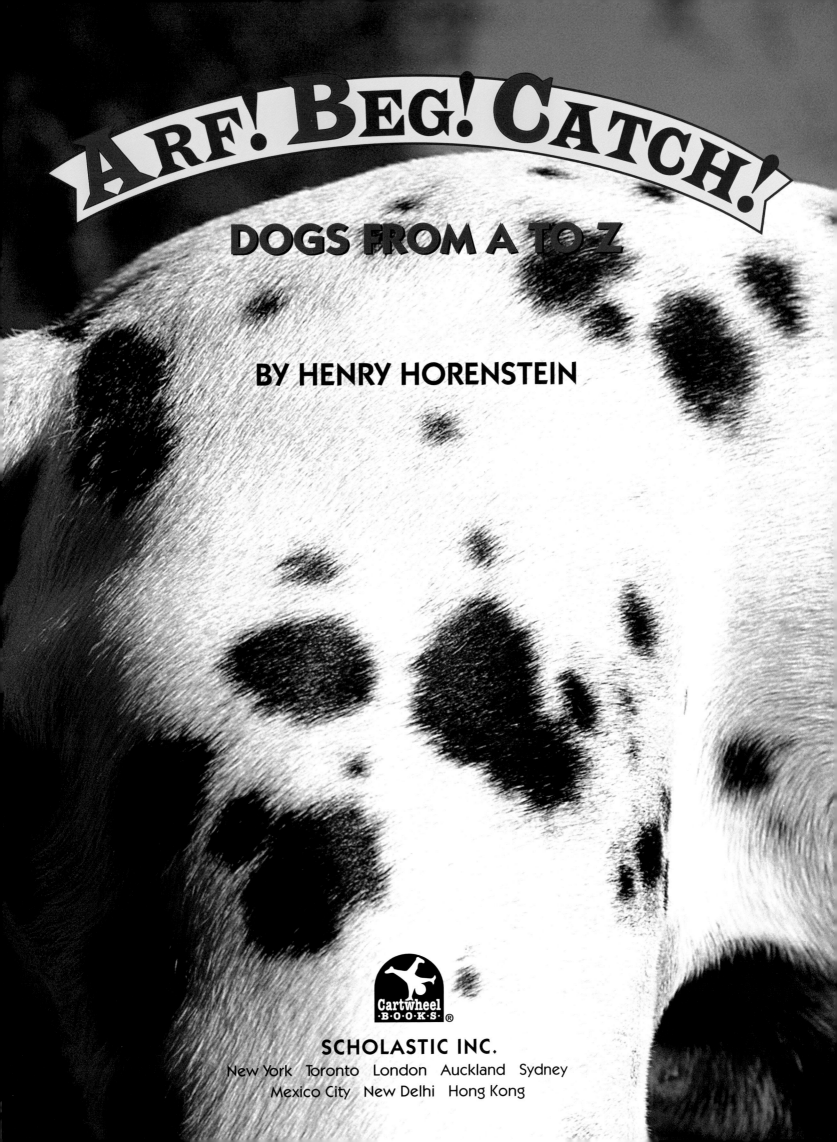

ARF! BEG! CATCH!

DOGS FROM A TO Z

BY HENRY HORENSTEIN

Cartwheel
·B·O·O·K·S·®

SCHOLASTIC INC.
New York Toronto London Auckland Sydney
Mexico City New Delhi Hong Kong

Aa

Arf!

Bb

beg

catch

Dd

drink

Ee

ears

Ff

friends

Gg

Good dog!

Hh

hairy

itchy

Jj

jump

Kk

kiss

Ll

litter

Mm

mutt

Nn

nose

over

Pp

puppy

Qq

quick

Rr

ride

sit

Ss

Tt

tail

Uu

up

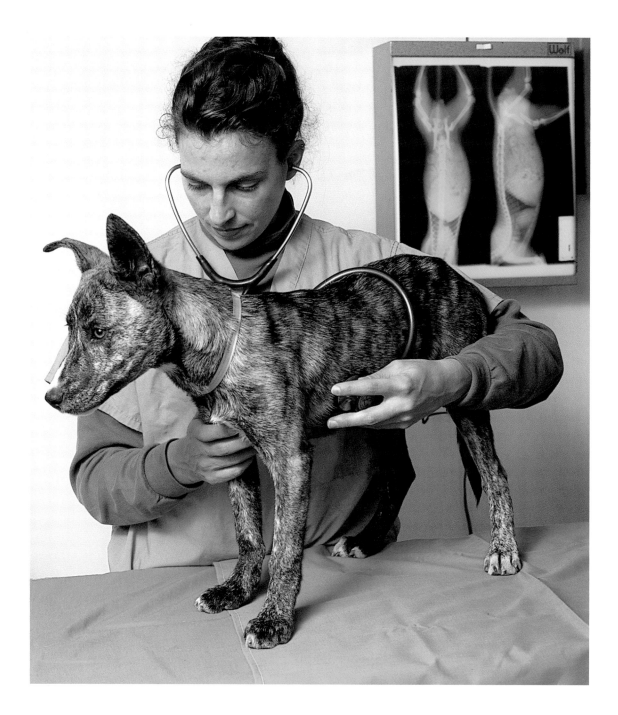

vet

Ww

wet

Xx

x-ray

yawn

Zz

Z-z-z-z

Library of Congress Cataloging-in-Publication Data

Horenstein, Henry.
   Arf! beg! catch!: dogs from A to Z/Henry Horenstein.
      p. cm.
   "Cartwheel books."
   Summary: Labeled illustrations present words related in some way to dogs.
   ISBN 0-590-03380-8
   1. Dogs —Juvenile literature. 2. English language—Alphabet—Juvenile literature.
   [1. Dogs. 2. Alphabet.] I. Title.
SF426.5.H67 1999
636.7—dc21   98-41721
                                                                                                CIP
                                                                                                AC

12 11 10 9 8 7 6 5 4 3 2 1   9/9 0/0 01 02 03 04

                              Printed in Singapore   46
                              First printing, September 1999

Aa Bb Cc

Gg Hh Ii Jj

Oo Pp Qq

Uu Vv Ww

Dd Ee Ff

Kk Ll Mm Nn

Rr Ss Tt

Xx Yy Zz